Bob and Shirley
A Tale of Two Lobsters

by Harriet Ziefert

illustrated by Mavis Smith

HOUGHTON MIFFLIN   BOSTON

Bob and Shirley were lobster friends. Shirley was at least 40 years old. Bob was younger than Shirley. How much younger, no one knew.

Bob and Shirley lived a quiet life.
Their home was in the cool ocean waters
near Maine. They crawled together
along the ocean floor.

One day, Bob and Shirley were caught in a net. They were taken to Rhode Island. A worker put bands around their big claws.

Then Bob and Shirley were packed in a box with ice. They were trucked to New York. Bob and Shirley spent the night in a crate.

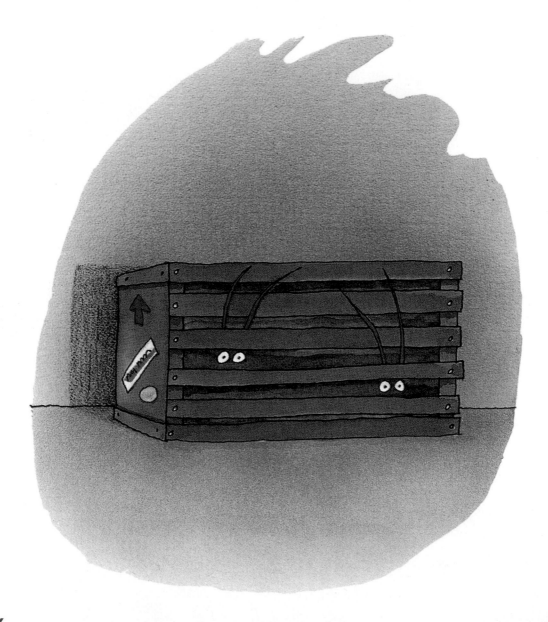

The next morning, they were packed again.
They were taken to a Philadelphia fish market.

The fish store owner proudly placed Bob
and Shirley in a big tank in his window.

Lots of people came to look at the two big lobsters from Maine.

At the end of the week, many people stood outside the fish market with signs.

The owner did not like having angry people outside his shop.

Bob and Shirley were packed in boxes again.

They were put on an airplane. They
were sent back to Maine.

   At the airport, they were loaded
onto a truck. They were driven to the dock.

A lobsterman picked up Bob by his tail.
He lifted Bob over the side of his boat.

Another lobsterman lifted Shirley onto
the same boat.

The lobsterman pulled away from the
dock. He headed toward the open sea.

After half an hour, he stopped. He cut
the bands from Bob's claws. He put him
back into the sea.

"He's a Maine lobster," the man said.
"This is where he belongs."

16

Then the lobsterman returned
Shirley to the sea.

Now Bob and Shirley were free
to swim side by side—perhaps for
another 40 years.